THE CALL OF THE WILD

Jack London
Retold by Sorrel Pitts

4

StandFor
graded readers

© 2016 – StandFor

Editorial Director	Lauri Cericato
Editorial Manager	Cayube Galas
Editorial Coordinator	Ana Carolina Costa Lopes
Series Editor	Nick Bullard
Editorial Assistant	Nathalia Thomaz
Production Manager	Mariana Milani
Production Coordinator	Marcelo Henrique Ferreira Fontes
Proofreader	Hannah Fish
Art Manager	Ricardo Borges
Art Coordinator	Daniela Di Creddo Máximo
Design	Yan Comunicação
Cover Design	Yan Comunicação
Art Supervisor	Patrícia De Michelis
Art Editors/Layout	Yan Comunicação, Lidiani Minoda
Illustrations Coordinator	Márcia Berne
Illustrations	Marcelo Camacho
Operations Director and Print Production Manager	Reginaldo Soares Damasceno

Dados Internacionais de Catalogação na Publicação (CIP)
(Câmara Brasileira do Livro, SP, Brasil)

Pitts, Sorrel
 The call of the wild : standfor graded readers, level 4 / Jack London ; retold by Sorrel Pitts ; Illustrated by Marcelo Camacho. -- 1. ed. -- São Paulo : FTD, 2016.

 ISBN 978-85-96-00428-2 (aluno)
 ISBN 978-85-96-00723-8 (professor)

 1. Literatura infantojuvenil I. London, Jack. II. Camacho, Marcelo. III. Título.

16-04251   CDD-028.5

Índices para catálogo sistemático:

1. Literatura infantil   028.5
2. Literatura infantojuvenil   028.5

All rights reserved. No part of this publication may be reproduced, stored in a retrieval system, or transmitted, in any form or by any means, electronic, mechanical, photocopying, recording, or otherwise, without the prior written permission of StandFor.

This book is sold subject to the condition that it shall not, by way of trade or otherwise, be lent, resold, hired out, or otherwise circulated without the publisher's prior consent in any form of binding or cover than that in which it is published and without a similar condition being imposed on the subsequent purchaser.

Rua Rui Barbosa, 156 – Bela Vista – São Paulo-SP – Brasil – CEP 01326-010
Phone 0800 772 2300 – Caixa Postal 65149 – CEP 01390-970 – www.standfor.com.br

Impresso no Parque Gráfico da Editora FTD
Avenida Antonio Bardella, 300 – Guarulhos-SP – CEP 07220-020
Tel. (11) 3545-8600 e Fax (11) 2412-5375

1 2 3 4 5 6 7 8 9

A - 604.922/20

THE CALL OF THE WILD

Jack London was born in San Francisco in 1876. He traveled to Dawson City in the Yukon, in Northern Canada at the age of 21 to look for gold, and when he returned to California he decided to try and write for a living. He used his experience in the Yukon in many of his stories which he sold to a number of magazines. He finished writing *Call of the Wild* in 1903, and it was an immediate success. However, London's health was not good, partly because of the hard times he had lived in the Yukon, and he died in California in 1916.

BEFORE READING

1 Look at the picture on the cover of the book. What kind of dog is this? Where do you usually see this kind of dog?

_____

2 Match the words with the pictures.

1. mountain
2. wolf
3. husky
4. whip
5. sled

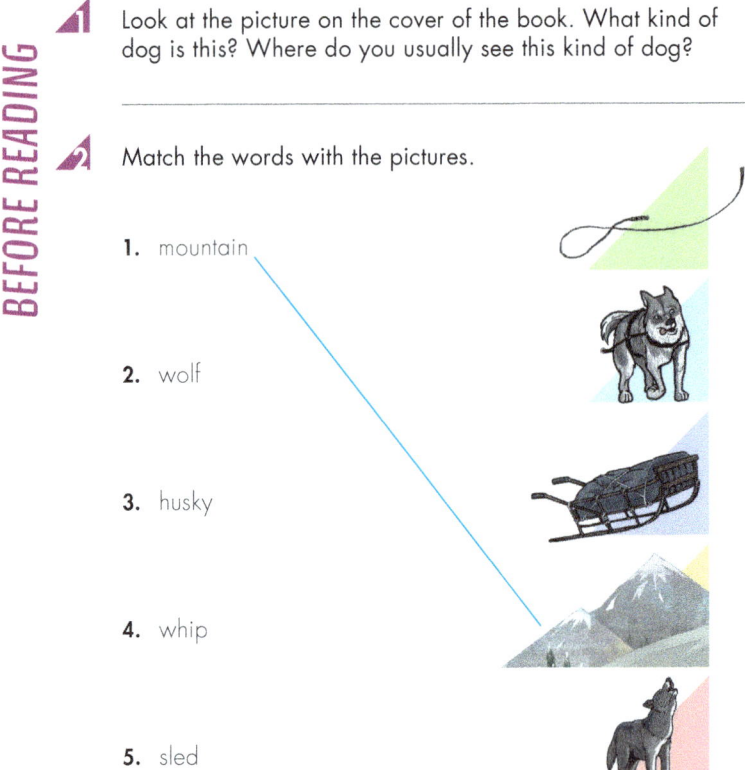

3 What do you know about the Klondike Gold Rush. Use the Internet to help you answer the questions.

1. When did the Klondike Gold Rush happen?

_____

2. Why did it happen?

_____

3. How many people went to the Klondike?

_____

4. What problems did they have?

_____

Chapter 1

Into the Wild

Buck had a good life with Mr. Miller and his family. He lived in a big house in California, where the sun was always shining. The house had wide gardens which were circled by tall trees.

Mr. Miller had other dogs of course, but four-year-old Buck was the biggest and the most beautiful – and he knew it. Buck was king of Mr. Miller's place. He could go in the house and outside in the gardens. He liked to run after small animals in the garden, and he loved swimming in its big pool.

Buck's father was a very big dog. His mother was smaller but she was very smart and fast. Buck wasn't as big as his father, but he was still very strong and could carry Mr. Miller's sons on his back.

But Buck didn't know that things were changing in the world. Men were looking for gold in the Yukon – in the north of Canada – and they needed dogs to help them find it. He also didn't know that Manuel, one of Mr. Miller's gardeners, was not a good man. Manuel liked to bet, and now he needed a lot of money.

Mr. Miller was out when Manuel put a rope around Buck's neck and took him quietly away through the garden. Buck didn't think much about this – he just thought he was going for a walk. When he saw Manuel meet a stranger, and accept money from him, he still didn't question it.

"If he gives you trouble just pull the rope hard," said Manuel.

Into the Wild | Chapter 1

Buck thought this was strange, but he knew Manuel and wasn't worried. But when the other man took the rope from Manuel, he growled nervously. The man pulled the rope hard and Buck became frightened. But each time he fought against the man or growled, the rope was pulled harder around his neck until Buck fell down on the floor and everything went black.

He woke up in a wooden box on a train. It was dark and there were strange noises which went on for two days and nights. Buck began to feel very hungry and thirsty.

When the train finally arrived at Seattle, four men took his box down from the train. A minute later, a strong man in a red shirt came. He was carrying a big club. He looked down at Buck and smiled.

"Are you going to do it now?" asked one of the four men in a nervous voice.

"Of course," said the man in the red shirt.

When he opened the door of Buck's box, the other men quickly moved away. Buck growled loudly and ran at the man. Suddenly his head was hurting badly and he fell to the ground.

Buck quickly climbed back to his feet. He was feeling very angry now, but each time he tried to bite the man he was hit by the club. It was no good. His head hurt and he couldn't see very well. Finally he lay down. He understood now that he could never win against a man with a club.

As the days went by, more dogs arrived with men and ropes. Some of the dogs were angry, and each time Buck watched the man in the red shirt hit them with the club. Then different men came, money changed hands, and the dogs were taken away.

One day, a small man with a thin face came to visit. His name was Perrault.

"That's one big, angry dog!" he said. "How much do you want for him?"

"Three hundred dollars – and that's cheap," said the man in the red shirt.

Perrault smiled. Dogs were becoming very expensive and it wasn't a lot of money. But Perrault also understood dogs, and he knew that Buck was very special.

Buck watched Perrault give money to the man in the red shirt. Then Perrault put ropes on Buck and another, smaller dog called Curly, and he took them down to a ship. There they were given to a large man called François. He took them down below where two other dogs waited. The first dog, Spitz, was white, and he was as big as Buck. He looked very friendly, but his eyes were strange and Buck didn't like him. The other dog, Dave, was quiet and wanted to be alone.

A few hours later, the ship's engines started and they pulled away from Seattle. Buck never saw the man in the red shirt, or Mr. Miller's house, again.

Days became nights and then days again. As the ship sailed more and more to the north, Buck felt that it was getting colder. Then, one morning, the ship's engines went quiet and there were excited voices outside. François put ropes on the dogs and took them upstairs. As Buck walked outside his feet touched something cold and white. He jumped with surprise. Then he put his head down, and licked carefully at the white ground. He heard the men. They were laughing at him and he felt stupid but didn't know why. It was his first snow.

Chapter 2
Buck Becomes a Sled Dog

François and Perrault were hard men, but they understood dogs and only hit them with a whip when it was needed. Buck didn't like these men, but he learned to respect them.

Life in the Yukon was very different from life at Mr. Miller's. It was cold and hard and there was no more sunshine or warm grass to sleep on. The other dogs were as hard and angry as the men, and there were often fights. Every second was dangerous. One morning, Buck saw a great husky jump on Curly and cut her face from eye to mouth. She fell, and then many dogs jumped on her. François and Perrault came with their clubs but it was too late – Curly was dead. Buck understood now. If you fell down in a fight, you were dead.

The Call off the Wild

That was his first surprise. The second was when François put a harness on him and made him work. He and the other dogs had to pull François on a sled to get wood for the fire. It was new and strange, but he learned quickly that "mush" meant "go" and "ho" meant "stop". Spitz was made the leader of the team because he was experienced and knew how to pull a sled.

That afternoon, Perrault brought two more huskies called Billee and Joe. Billee was friendly but Joe was quiet and unhappy. The next dog to join them was called Sol-leks, which means "the angry one". Sol-leks was always angry because he could only see from one eye. That night, Buck learned about sleeping in the cold. He learned that the men didn't want him near their fires, so he watched the other dogs make their beds under the snow and he decided to copy them. He was surprised and happy when his body quickly warmed the snow around him. Soon he was sleeping deeply.

Three more huskies came the next morning and finally the team was in harness and ready to travel the trail to Dawson. Buck was put between Dave and Sol-leks because both were experienced sled dogs and they could teach him.

Buck Becomes a Sled Dog | Chapter 2

When Buck did something wrong he got a bite, so he soon learned to copy everything Dave and Sol-leks did.

On the first day, the team traveled seventy kilometers. The snow on the mountains was hard and the trail was fast. But the next days were slower because the snow was deep and soft. Each night the men made a camp and gave the dogs food, but there was never enough, and Buck was always hungry. He soon learned to eat his food quickly or another dog could take it from him. One night, he watched Pike, one of the new dogs, take a small piece of meat when Perrault wasn't looking. The next day he copied Pike and took a much larger piece of meat. He was quick and the men didn't see him. They thought it was Dub, a smaller, slower dog, and he – not Buck – got the whip.

The Call of the Wild

Life in the Yukon was making Buck a stronger, healthier dog. His body was thin and hard, and he was becoming quick and smart. He felt different, too. He didn't know it, but he was remembering his ancestors – the dogs and wolves who lived many years ago and didn't know any men. He just knew that it felt good for him to bite and fight, or lift his nose and howl loudly at the moon.

As life on the trail continued, the call of Buck's ancestors grew stronger. Buck didn't want to fight Spitz because he was learning to be wise and to think carefully. But Spitz didn't like this new, smart Buck and he showed it by growling or trying to bite him. He was the dogs' leader and he wanted Buck to know it.

Buck Becomes a Sled Dog | Chapter 2

One night, after a very hard day, Buck made his usual hole in the snow. He was very tired when he got up to eat his dinner. When he came back, Spitz was lying in his warm hole. Buck was exhausted and angry, and he opened his mouth and barked loudly before jumping on Spitz and biting him. Spitz barked back and ran at Buck. The men were soon between them with their clubs. But after that day, there was a lot of trouble between the two dogs. Both were waiting for the next chance to fight.

Chapter 3

A Fight to the End

Perrault was worried. Buck and Spitz were tired after their fight and it was still 700 kilometers to Dawson. And he knew that now they had to travel the most difficult part of the trail.

The Thirty Mile River was wide and dangerous; it had fast moving water and the ice was very thin in places. It took the team six days to travel fifty kilometers along it. Perrault walked in front of the team to check the ice and he nearly fell through it many times. Another time, Spitz and half the team went through the ice and into the water. Luckily, Dave, Buck, and François were strong enough to pull them back. Another time, the ice broke and the only way out was to climb a mountain above the river. The men pulled the dogs up on a rope. Then they had to come back down to the river. On that day, they only traveled a kilometer.

The Call of the Wild

A few days later, they came to good, strong ice. The dogs were still tired from climbing the mountain above the river but Perrault woke them up early and that day they traveled fifty kilometers.

Buck's feet were not as hard as the huskies', and they became sore. Soon he began to limp so François made four small boots and this helped him – and made the men smile.

But not all the dogs could continue with this hard life. One morning, as the men were putting the harness on them, Dolly, who was usually quiet, suddenly lifted her nose and howled loudly. Then she jumped at Buck and tried to bite him. Buck could see something was very wrong, and he quickly ran away from her. Dolly followed him with red eyes. Buck was frightened and didn't know what to do, so he ran and ran until he heard Perrault call him. Then Buck turned back with Dolly after him. When he ran past Perrault, the man lifted an ax and brought it down hard on Dolly's head.

Buck was exhausted and lay down on the ground to rest. Now Spitz saw his chance and the next second he jumped on Buck and bit his neck and throat. Then Buck heard the sound of the whip and Spitz jumped back.

"That Spitz is a devil," said Perrault. "He's going to kill Buck one day."

A Fight to the End | Chapter 3

"But Buck is two devils," said François. "He's going to kill Spitz and leave him in small pieces on the snow."

But Buck didn't have his chance to fight Spitz before the team arrived in Dawson. There, the dogs relaxed for seven days. But then the team was back on the trail towards the ocean. Perrault wanted to travel fast. He knew that the dogs were rested and the sled was light. The snow was also hard because many other teams were traveling along it in front of them. Perrault saw this was a great chance to break a record time and win some money.

The team was flying along. On the first day they went eighty kilometers and at the end of the second they were a hundred and sixty kilometers up the Yukon. But François was having a lot of trouble with the dogs because they still remembered the fight between Spitz and Buck, and now they didn't respect their leader. All the dogs started to make trouble with Spitz in small ways. One day, Pike took a piece of fish from him when he wasn't looking. Another evening, Dub and Joe fought him and he couldn't fight back because there were two of them. Buck was the worst. He liked to come near Spitz and growl angrily, then walk around him with his head high.

The Call of the Wild

François knew that Buck was the problem, but he could do nothing to stop it. Buck was too smart. He worked hard in his harness – he liked the work now – and François never saw him growl or bite Spitz so he couldn't stop him with the whip.

Then, one night after dinner, a rabbit ran past the dogs. Seconds later, they were all running after it with loud howls. Buck was the leader, but he couldn't catch the rabbit because it could run fast and light over the heavy snow. Buck could smell the rabbit's blood and he heard the call of his ancestors and the wild dogs that came before men. He felt this and ran faster through the deep snow with the other dogs behind him.

Spitz saw his chance and turned through some trees. He knew the trail which Buck and the team were following. It soon came back around the trees, and he planned to meet them on the other side. Buck didn't see him go, and as he came along the trail with the rabbit in front of him, Spitz suddenly jumped out of the trees and onto the rabbit. The rabbit couldn't turn and Buck watched Spitz bite down and break its neck.

A Fight to the End | Chapter 3

Buck didn't bark or growl. He ran at Spitz and pushed him hard, but the white dog met him shoulder to shoulder and they fell together into the snow. They jumped up again and circled each other. Then they started growling loudly. In a second, Buck understood. This was going to be a fight to the end.

Spitz was strong and he was the winner of many fights. He was very angry, but he was smart, too. He never forgot that other dogs wanted to kill him and he knew that he had to wait and watch until he was ready.

The other dogs lay in the snow and watched quietly. Each time Buck tried to bite the neck of the big white dog, Spitz's teeth were there first. Tooth hit tooth, and soon both dogs' mouths had blood on them. Sometimes Buck ran at Spitz and tried to push him down, but Spitz bit Buck's shoulder and jumped away. Buck had a long cut on his shoulder and many cuts on his legs, but Spitz didn't have any cuts; the only blood on him was Buck's. Now Spitz was running at Buck and Buck nearly went down. The other dogs stood up quickly and waited for the kill. But Buck quickly climbed back on his feet so they lay back down again.

Spitz was smart, but Buck was smarter. He ran at Spitz and suddenly his body went low and his teeth closed around Spitz's leg. There was the sound of breaking bone and now the white dog was standing on three legs. Buck did the same thing again. Now two legs were broken. As Spitz fought on, the other dogs quietly moved forward.

Buck jumped forward and his shoulder met Spitz's body. Spitz barked loudly, then he turned and limped quickly away over the snow.

Buck stood with his head high when the other dogs came to meet him. He was the leader of the team now, and they knew it.

Chapter 4
All Work and No Rest

"That Spitz is a devil," said Perrault the next day when he found Buck. "Look at these cuts."

"But Buck has won!" replied François. "This is good. No more Spitz and no more trouble. Now we can travel faster."

When Perrault packed the sled and François started putting the dogs in harness, Buck quickly ran to Spitz's place at the front of the team.

"Now Buck wants to be leader!" said François. He pulled Buck away and put the harness on Sol-leks. But Buck growled and ran at Sol-leks, who looked frightened.

"Get away you devil!" said François, and he went to get the club. Buck remembered the man in the red shirt and moved away. But he continued to circle and growl. And when François called Buck and tried to put him in his usual place in the team, he didn't move. François stepped towards him with the club in his hand, but Buck jumped away again. This went on for more than an hour. Perrault and François shouted at Buck and threw their clubs at him, but he continued to growl and circle, and they couldn't catch him.

Perrault looked at his watch with a worried face. It was late in the morning now and he wanted to be on the trail.

"OK, Buck," said François finally, and he went up to Sol-leks and took off his harness before moving him back to his usual place. Buck watched but didn't move.

"Throw down your club!" shouted Perrault.

So François dropped the club and Buck quickly ran to the front of the team with his head held high. François put on his harness and a second later they were back on the trail.

Dave and Sol-leks were not worried about their change of leader. They knew their job was only to work hard

in their harnesses and to travel fast. But some of the other dogs were surprised when Buck made them work harder and run faster than before. François saw that he had an excellent lead dog in Buck. He didn't think it was possible, but Buck was a better leader than Spitz.

There was no more trouble between dogs in the team. They ran fast and well together behind Buck, and didn't need to stop very often. They were in front of the record and the trail was good because there was no new snow and it stayed very cold. When they arrived back at the Thirty Mile River it was thick with ice and they traveled quickly. After that, they ran for a hundred kilometers to the White Horse Rapids. And after only two weeks they arrived in Skagway and saw the lights of the ships.

Buck and the team were the fastest sled team ever to run between Dawson and Skagway. The record was broken, and Perrault and François ate, drank, and slept for the next three days while the dogs rested.

But life went on and new orders came for the men. François put his arms around Buck and cried, and then he and Perrault left Buck's life for ever.

A Scottish man called Jimmy bought Buck and the team. With twelve other dogs and many men, they were the mail carriers, taking letters and boxes to the people who were looking for gold. This time there was no more light running, or records to break. Every day was the same. In the morning, fires were made and breakfast was cooked. Then the dogs were put in harness and they started on the trail. When it became dark, camp was made. One man cut wood for the fire, while another gave the dogs their dinner.

All the dogs loved this part of the day. Buck liked to rest by the big fire with his nose on his feet. Sometimes he thought about Mr. Miller's big house in California and the other dogs he knew there. But he didn't miss his old home, and he thought more often about the fight with Spitz and the cold mountains and forests which brought the call of his ancestors.

Buck soon became the leader of the new dogs, too. Some of them could fight, but he stood tall and barked and they quickly became frightened and moved away.

All Work and No Rest | Chapter 4

The work was much harder with these men. The sled was always heavy with mail, and the dogs soon became really tired. But when they arrived in Dawson they were only given two days' rest and then they started back again. This time the sled was even heavier and it snowed every day, which made the trail slow and difficult. The men tried to help the dogs – at camp they always got their food first and their feet were checked – but they were becoming weak and tired. Billee cried all the time, Joe was quiet and sad, and Sol-leks was even angrier than before.

But Dave was the worst. Something was wrong with him and he didn't want to be with the other dogs. He was quiet and unhappy and each evening he quickly went and made his bed in the snow after eating his dinner. Sometimes, when he was in his harness, he cried out – something was hurting him badly. The men brought him to the fire and checked his body and feet, but they couldn't find anything wrong.

One day on the trail, Dave fell down. Jimmy stopped the dogs and took him out of his harness to rest. Sol-leks was put in his place but this made Dave growl and look even more unhappy. He didn't want to be out of his harness because he was proud of his work and he wanted to stay in the team. When the sled started again, he ran at Sol-leks and tried to bite him. Jimmy hit him with the whip but it didn't stop him, and the man felt bad and didn't want to hit him harder. Dave ran and bit and barked until the sled stopped again. Then he went and stood next to Sol-leks.

All Work and No Rest | Chapter 4

Jimmy looked down at Dave with worried eyes. Then another man, Thomas, told him about dogs who were too weak to work but didn't want to leave their harnesses.

"He wants to die at work," he said.

So Jimmy put the harness back on Dave and they traveled on to camp. But the next morning Dave was very weak and he couldn't climb to his feet. The team could hear him crying behind them as they followed the trail around some trees. Then the sled stopped; Jimmy left it and walked back behind the trees. The next moment there was the sound of a gun. The other dogs didn't look back because they all knew that Dave was dead.

Chapter 5

Buck Meets John Thornton

Thirty days after leaving Dawson, the team was back in Skagway. The dogs were thin and exhausted and their feet were sore. Pike and Dub were limping and Sol-leks had a bad shoulder. Every part of their bodies ached and they needed rest.

The men were tired, too and they hoped to relax in Skagway. But they soon saw the thousands of letters and boxes which were waiting for the people on the trail, and then the order came. They had to take the mail to Dawson as soon as possible.

After three days, the dogs were still too tired to go back on the trail, so the mail carriers bought new dogs. But there was no time to rest for Buck and his team. On the fourth day, two men came and bought them. Their names were Hal and Charles. Charles was forty years old and he had light hair. Hal was younger and his face was thin and hard. Both wore expensive clothes and they were different from the other men of the North.

Buck watched money change hands and understood that now Jimmy was leaving his life, too. The new men took him and the other dogs to their camp where a small woman waited for them. The men called her "Mercedes" and she was Charles' wife and Hal's sister.

Clothes, food, and other camping things lay on the ground around them. Buck felt worried as he watched the men put everything on the sled. He knew it was much too high and heavy. Then Charles brought the dogs to the sled and put them in harness.

Two other men came and watched. They soon began laughing quietly because they guessed that this was Hal and Charles' first visit to the Yukon. They were not experienced on the trail and did not know what they were doing.

"You've put too much on that sled," said one of the men. "You'll need to take that tent off."

"No!" said Mercedes, and she put her hands to her mouth. "How can I sleep without a tent?"

"It's spring, so it won't be very cold," replied the man.

But Mercedes argued loudly and the tent stayed on the sled.

"Mush!" shouted Hal, and he lifted the whip. The dogs pulled hard, but the sled didn't move.

"Mush!" he said again, and this time the whip came down on their bodies.

"Oh, Hal, no!" said Mercedes. "Please don't hit them! If you hit them again, I won't come with you."

"You know nothing about dogs," replied Hal. "You need to whip them to make them go."

"Those dogs are weak," said one of the men who was watching. "They're tired from traveling and they need rest."

But Hal didn't listen. "Mush!" he shouted, and he hit the dogs a second time. They pulled as hard as they could but they still couldn't move the sled.

"If you take some boxes off that sled, it will help," said the man.

The third time Hal tried, the sled broke free from the ice and the dogs began to run. The sled was suddenly flying over the snow and it surprised Hal. "Slow!" he shouted, but the dogs were angry and he couldn't stop them. The next second, the sled turned and fell, and the tent, clothes, and food were thrown across the snow.

Buck Meets John Thornton | Chapter 5

People came to help. They collected the things and brought them back to the sled. "It needs to be much lighter, and you need more dogs," they said.

Hal and Charles listened unhappily, but they started taking things off the sled and Charles went to buy six new dogs.

Hal and Charles smiled as they started on the trail with a lighter sled and fourteen dogs. It was a very big team and they felt proud and smart. Mercedes walked behind them and she was smiling, too. But the men who watched knew that taking fourteen dogs was stupid – the sled couldn't carry enough dog food for them.

Buck led the team but he didn't feel proud. The six new dogs were unhappy because they weren't used to this cold hard life and men who used the whip. The old team were exhausted and didn't want to work. He also knew that the two men and the woman were no good and couldn't learn. It took them many hours each night to make camp and many more hours each morning to put everything back on the sled. Some days the team traveled no more than fifteen kilometers.

Soon there was not enough dog food. The new dogs were always hungry and during the first

week the men gave them too much to eat. Then they gave them too little and the dogs from Buck's old team became even thinner and weaker. The first to go was Dub. His shoulder still ached and he limped badly. One morning, Hal took out his gun and killed him. The new dogs were next because they were not used to working so hard and eating so little. Mercedes cried but she couldn't stop Hal from killing them.

The hard life on the trail was hurting the people, too. They were unhappy and exhausted and their bodies ached. Soon Mercedes stopped crying about the dogs and started shouting at her husband and brother. Then the men started arguing because Hal thought he worked harder than Charles, and Charles thought he worked harder than Hal. Sometimes they argued all evening and the camp wasn't ready before night came.

Mercedes became a problem, too, because she was used to an easy life and getting the things she wanted. "I want to ride on the sled," she said one day. It was too much for the exhausted dogs, who soon fell in their harnesses. The men tried to pull her from the sled but she sat down in the snow and didn't move until they came back and lifted her back onto it.

They continued along the trail. Buck tried his best and pulled when he could, but sometimes he fell down because he was so weak. The other dogs were the same. There were only seven of them now and they were too tired to feel the whip and the club on their backs. When Hal told them to stop, they fell in the snow and lay without moving.

One morning Billee fell and didn't get up again, so Hal killed him with an ax. Another dog fell on the trail, and now there were just Buck, Joe, Pike, Teek, and Sol-leks in the team.

Spring was coming and the sun shone each day. Leaves were growing on the trees and small rivers came down from the mountains. It was very beautiful but the people and dogs were exhausted and they didn't have time to look. Mercedes and the men continued to argue. They were still arguing when the tired, unhappy dogs slowly pulled the sled into John Thornton's camp, at the mouth of White River.

There they stopped, and the dogs fell down on the ground. Mercedes looked at John Thornton. He was sitting down on a piece of wood and repairing an ax with slow, careful, hands. He listened quietly while Hal talked. Sometimes he said one or two wise words but he knew that the men didn't want to listen to him.

"Don't go on the ice, it's too thin," he told them. "If you go on it, it will break."

"It's spring and there isn't much snow. But we have followed the trail. People said it was impossible to get to White River but we are here. And now we can cross it," Hal replied proudly.

"Then you are stupid," said John Thornton.

"And you're not stupid?" said Hal. "Well thank you for your help, but we will go on to Dawson. "Mush, Buck! Mush!"

But the dogs didn't want to move. The whip came down hard and Sol-leks finally climbed to his feet. Teek and Joe followed but Pike stood and then quickly fell down again. Buck didn't even try. The whip came down on him again and again, but he didn't cry or move. John Thornton watched without speaking, but water came into his eyes. Then he stood and started walking slowly up and down.

Hal was very angry now. He dropped the whip and started hitting Buck with the club. But Buck felt strongly that something was wrong and he didn't want to cross the ice. The club came down hard on his body again and again.

Suddenly there was a loud shout and John Thornton jumped on Hal and threw him back, hard. Mercedes screamed and began to cry. Charles watched quietly but didn't stand or help because he was tired and his body ached.

"If you hit that dog again, I'll kill you," John Thornton said.

"It's my dog," replied Hal. "Now, we're going to Dawson."

The Call of the Wild

Buck Meets John Thornton | Chapter 5

Thornton stood between Hal and Buck. Hal slowly took out a long knife but Thornton quickly hit his hand with the ax and the knife fell to the ground. Mercedes screamed again. Then Thornton took the knife and quickly cut Buck from his harness. Hal was too tired to fight and he could see that Buck was no good to pull the sled. A few minutes later the two men and the woman pulled away from the camp and went down to the river. Pike was the leader and Sol-leks was at the back. Between them were Joe and Teek. They were limping and falling. Mercedes was riding on the sled with Hal in front and Charles behind.

John Thornton put his hand on Buck's back and felt his body for broken bones.

The sled was at the river now. Buck and Thornton watched it slowly pull out onto the ice. Suddenly they saw the ice open and the sled drop into the water. They saw Charles turn and try to run back while Mercedes screamed. Then suddenly the sled, dogs, and people all fell into the water.

John Thornton looked down at Buck.

"You poor devil," he said, and Buck licked his hand.

Chapter 6
For Love and Gold

When John Thornton hurt his feet the year before, his friends left him at the camp and went on to Dawson. They needed a boat to carry them down the river, and Thornton was waiting for them to come back.

Thornton was still limping when Charles and Hal's team arrived, but it was getting warmer, and soon he could walk easily. Buck didn't have to do anything but rest each day in the sunshine next to the river, and he became strong and well again, too.

Thornton had two other dogs – Skeet and Soot. Skeet was small and friendly and she always wanted to help Buck. Each day she came to him and licked his cuts. Soot was big and black. He had soft eyes and he liked to play with Buck.

Mr. Miller was Buck's friend, but Buck didn't know love until he met John Thornton. For Thornton, dogs were the same as children. He loved to sit and talk to them, and sometimes he would put Buck's head in his hands and say soft words to him. Then Buck liked to take John Thornton's hand in his mouth and move it from side to side. Thornton knew it was Buck's way of showing him his love.

Buck didn't like it when he couldn't see Thornton, so he always followed him around the camp. He was used to men leaving his life and he was frightened, because he didn't want to lose Thornton. At night, he slept next to the tent so he could listen to Thornton sleeping.

But sometimes when Buck lay next to the campfire, he heard strange sounds coming from the forest which excited him greatly. Sometimes he got up and followed the sounds through the forest before coming back to camp in the morning. He didn't know it, but his ancestors were calling him again, and he was answering them.

But his love for Thornton always brought him back to the camp. When Pete and Hans arrived on the boat and took them back to Dawson, Buck didn't go near them until he was sure they were Thornton's friends.

His love for Thornton became deeper and stronger. Later that year on the fast water of the Forty Mile River, Thornton fell from the boat into the water. Pete and Hans put a rope on Buck's body. Buck jumped into the water and Thornton held his neck. Buck swam for the side of the river but the water was too wild and fast and it threw him and Thornton against the rocks. Hans and Pete pulled the rope hard, bringing Buck and Thornton back on to dry ground. Buck lay on the ground as Skeet licked his eyes and face. He had long cuts on his body and three of his bones were broken.

"Right," said Thornton. "We'll camp here until he's better."

That winter, at Dawson, Buck did another great thing. Thornton, Pete, and Hans were drinking in a bar with some men when they all started talking about their favorite dogs.

"I had a dog who could pull a sled with two hundred kilograms on it," said a man called Matthewson.

"That's nothing," replied Thornton. "Buck can pull a sled with four hundred kilograms on it."

"And walk for a hundred meters?" replied Matthewson.

"Yes," said Thornton. "And walk for a hundred meters."

"I don't believe you. I'll bet you a thousand dollars that he can't do it." Matthewson took out a bag of gold and put it on the table.

For a second both men were quiet. Thornton's face was hot and he was worried. Buck was a strong dog but could he really pull four hundred kilograms? Thornton didn't know and he didn't want to look stupid. More importantly, he didn't have a thousand dollars.

"I've got a sled outside now with four hundred kilograms of food on it," continued Matthewson. "So we don't need to wait."

Thornton turned and looked at the men around him. Next to him stood Jim O'Brien, an experienced trail man and an old friend.

"Do you have one thousand dollars, Jim?" he said quietly.

"Of course," replied O'Brien, and he put a bag down next to Matthewson's. "But I don't think he can do it, John."

All the men came out of the bar to stand on the street outside. Some started to bet. Most of them thought Buck wasn't strong enough to pull the sled and they bet against him.

Matthewson's sled stood on the street outside in the snow and ice.

"The ice on the ground is holding the sled. He'll have to break that ice first," said Matthewson in an excited voice. "I'll bet you another thousand that he can't do it."

Thornton, Hans, and Pete put their hands in their pockets. Together they had only two hundred dollars. It was all their money. But Thornton was proud and he put it down in front of Matthewson without speaking.

Matthewson's huskies were taken out of their harness and Buck was put in front of the sled. Thornton put his hand on his dog's head. "I love you and you love me," he said quietly. Then Thornton stepped back and the men went quiet.

"Now Buck," Thornton said and Buck pushed forward. First he pulled to the left, and then to the right, because he was experienced at pulling sleds from ice. "Mush!" shouted Thornton, and Buck pulled forward hard. There was a loud noise, and suddenly the sled broke free from the ice. Buck's head and body were low. He pulled again and the sled slowly began to move. Then it moved faster and faster until Buck was running and the sled was flying over the ice and snow!

The men shouted and the noise got louder and louder. Thornton was running behind the sled and calling to Buck. The sled was moving faster and faster. "Forty meters, seventy meters, one hundred meters!" the men shouted. There were cries and screams. Hats and gloves flew in the air and the men started dancing in the street. They couldn't believe it!

John Thornton dropped down next to Buck and put his arms around his neck. The other men heard him say soft words to his dog. Then Buck took Thornton's hand in his mouth and moved his head from side to side.

Chapter 7

The Final Call

Thornton, Hans, and Pete knew about a camp in the far east of the Yukon where there was a lot of gold. Now they had the money from Thornton's bet, they decided to find it.

They traveled for two winters and a summer; up the Yukon, then along the Stewart River past the Mayo, and into the high mountains. John Thornton and the other men were happy and relaxed in the wild. They lived a simple life and used their guns to kill animals for meat or caught fish from the rivers.

Buck loved traveling through these strange places. Sometimes they pulled the sled for many weeks, and sometimes they stopped and camped for days while the men washed their clothes and made fires. Often the men and their dogs were hungry, but at other times there was too much food to eat.

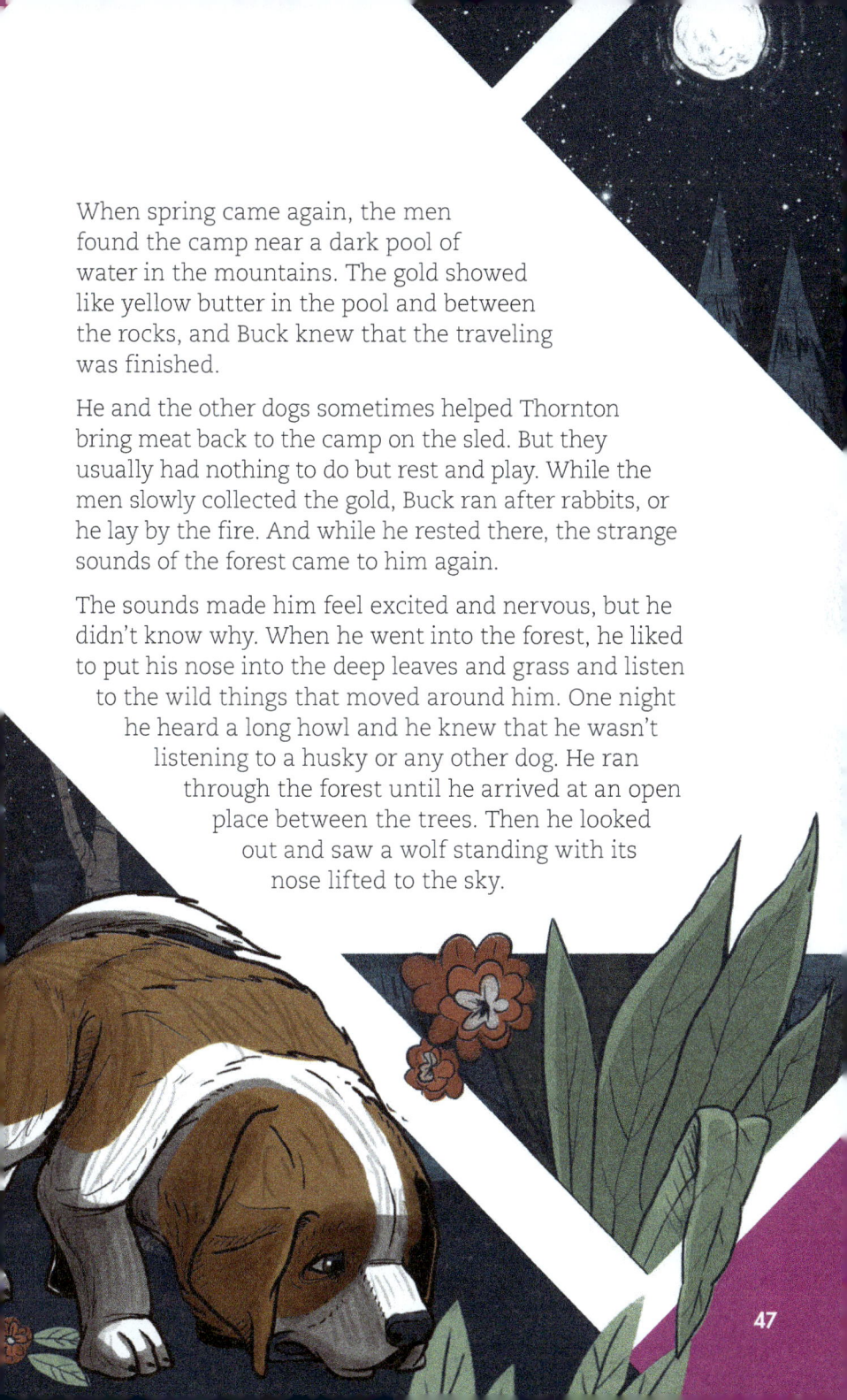

When spring came again, the men found the camp near a dark pool of water in the mountains. The gold showed like yellow butter in the pool and between the rocks, and Buck knew that the traveling was finished.

He and the other dogs sometimes helped Thornton bring meat back to the camp on the sled. But they usually had nothing to do but rest and play. While the men slowly collected the gold, Buck ran after rabbits, or he lay by the fire. And while he rested there, the strange sounds of the forest came to him again.

The sounds made him feel excited and nervous, but he didn't know why. When he went into the forest, he liked to put his nose into the deep leaves and grass and listen to the wild things that moved around him. One night he heard a long howl and he knew that he wasn't listening to a husky or any other dog. He ran through the forest until he arrived at an open place between the trees. Then he looked out and saw a wolf standing with its nose lifted to the sky.

Buck was not making any noise, but the wolf stopped howling and turned to watch him. Then he quickly ran into the trees. Buck followed him until they came to a river. The wolf suddenly jumped from side to side, then he turned and showed his teeth to Buck.

Buck didn't try to fight. He circled slowly, always friendly, but the wolf soon started running again. Buck ran with him, shoulder to shoulder. Finally the wolf stopped and turned. They touched noses and began to play.

After a minute, the wolf went on and Buck followed. Hour after hour they ran, through forests and mountains. The sun lifted in the sky and the day became warm. Buck was excited and happy because he was following the call of his ancestors and it felt good and true.

Finally they came to a river and stopped to drink. While he drank, Buck suddenly remembered John Thornton.

The thought made him sit down. Then he turned and started traveling back to the camp. The wolf followed him for more than an hour before it sat down, lifted its nose to the sky, and howled loudly.

John Thornton was eating dinner when Buck came back into the camp and jumped on him. He licked his face again and again and bit his hand hard. For the next two days he never left his side. He followed him while he worked and watched him while he ate and slept.

But after two days the call from the forest came again. Buck couldn't rest and he began to move around the camp. He couldn't stop thinking about his wild brothers and the beautiful places where they ran.

He started sleeping in the forest at night. Sometimes he traveled for three or four days. He killed animals for meat while he traveled,

The Final Call | Chapter 7

and caught big fish in the rivers. One night he killed a big black bear. The bear had a problem with its eyes and it couldn't see, but it was still a hard fight. Two days later Buck came back and found three wolves. They were eating the bear's body. He barked and jumped at them, and they ran into the forest.

Buck's need to kill grew stronger. He was a wild dog now, an animal which killed and ate other animals. And this made him feel proud and alive.

But one day after a long time away from camp, Buck came back to find everything was changed. First he saw Soot on the ground with a hole in his body. He was dead.

Buck moved forward quietly. Next he came to one of the sled dogs from Dawson. The husky was moving slowly on its back from side to side and it had blood on its head. Buck knew it was dying and he went past it without stopping.

Buck's body dropped low as he came near the tents because he could feel and smell that things were very wrong. The camp was strangely quiet. Then he saw Hans. He was lying on his front, with a pool of blood around his head. At the same time, he saw three or four strange men who were sitting by the tents. One man had a gun in his hand.

For the first time, Buck forgot to be smart. He didn't think, but simply jumped forward with a great bark onto the man with the gun, and bit into his neck. Blood ran down the man's body and in seconds he was dead. The other three men jumped up, but they didn't have guns with them. They screamed and ran into the trees.

Buck turned and went back to the camp. He saw clothes and food on the ground. Then he saw Skeet. She was lying with her head and feet in the water. Next to her lay John Thornton's dead body.

Buck sat by the river all day. He felt deeply sad. But he was also proud because the man with the gun was dead, and it was because of him.

Night came and the bright moon lifted in the sky. With the night came the sounds of the forest. Buck lifted his head and stood up. Then he slowly walked into the clear place in the forest and listened. John Thornton was dead and he knew that he didn't have to stay at the camp now. His life with men was finished.

The group of wolves came into the clear place under the light of the moon. Buck stood and waited for them. One ran at him and he bit it and threw it down. Then another jumped on him, but Buck was too strong. Buck could see the blood and cuts on their bodies. Finally the other wolves came at him together. Buck bit and jumped and circled until they all moved away with their long white teeth showing in the moonlight. Some stood and watched him quietly. Others lay down on the ground.

The Final Call | Chapter 7

Then, a long, thin wolf came forward. Buck stepped forward and touched its nose. It was his brother-wolf from before. Behind it came another, older wolf. Buck growled softly, then touched his nose, too. The next second, all the wolves sat down and howled loudly. When they were finished, they came around Buck and touched him with their noses and bodies. They were half friendly, and half angry. Suddenly the leaders of the group turned with a howl and ran into the trees. The other wolves and Buck followed them, shoulder to shoulder, into the wild.

WHILE READING ACTIVITIES

1
Read pages 5–15 and answer the questions.

1. Where is Buck living at the beginning of the story?
   California.

2. Why does Manuel take Buck?
   _____

3. What does Buck learn from the man in the red shirt?
   _____

4. How is Buck's life different in the Yukon to his life in California?
   _____

5. How does Buck feel about Perrault and François?
   _____

6. How does Buck change when he gets to the Yukon?
   _____

7. Who does Buck start to remember?
   _____

8. Which dog does Buck have a problem with in the team? Why is there a problem?
   _____

2
Read pages 16–22. Write the names of the person or animal.

1. This dog takes a small piece of meat from Spitz. ___Pike___

2. This dog is the leader of the team. He hates Buck. _____

3. This man makes four small boots for Buck. _____

4. This dog cannot continue living in the Yukon. She is killed with an ax. _____

5. This man wants to break a record and win some money.
   _____

6. The dogs want to eat this animal. _____

3) Read pages 23–29. Use one of these words to join the sentences together.

/ and   because   but /

1. François stepped towards him with the club in his hand, ___but___ Buck jumped away again.

2. He didn't think it was possible, _____ Buck was a better leader than Spitz.

3. Buck was the leader, but he couldn't catch the rabbit _____ it could run fast and light over the heavy snow.

4. Buck's feet were not as hard as the huskies', _____ they became sore.

5. But François was having a lot of trouble with the dogs _____ they still remembered the fight between Spitz and Buck.

6. Then Buck heard the sound of the whip _____ Spitz jumped back.

7. The snow was also hard _____ many other teams were traveling along it in front of them.

8. "He's going to kill Spitz _____ leave him in small pieces on the snow."

4) Read pages 30–39. Put these sentences in the correct order. Number them 1 through 8.

a. The team starts on the trail but Buck doesn't feel proud. ☐

b. Mercedes wants to ride on the sled. ☐

c. The team arrives at John Thornton's camp. ☐

d. The dogs are bought by two men who wear strange clothes. ☐

e. The dogs rest for three days. [1]

f. The sled falls over. ☐

g. The sled goes into the water. ☐

h. Hal fights with John Thornton. ☐

WHILE READING ACTIVITIES

5 Read pages 40–45 and check the best answer.

1. John Thornton was waiting at the camp because…
   a. his friends needed a boat. ☐
   b. his feet were hurt. ✓
   c. he liked being in the sunshine. ☐

2. John Thornton's two other dogs…
   a. were nice to Buck. ☐
   b. did not like Buck. ☐
   c. were the same as children. ☐

3. Buck loved John Thornton…
   a. as much as he loved Mr. Miller. ☐
   b. more than he loved Mr. Miller. ☐
   c. more than all men. ☐

4. Buck went into the forest because…
   a. he heard sounds and remembered his ancestors. ☐
   b. he couldn't sleep. ☐
   c. he was hungry. ☐

5. Buck went into the river because…
   a. he wanted to swim. ☐
   b. he wanted to help Thornton. ☐
   c. he fell from the boat. ☐

6. Thornton bet… that Buck could pull the sled.

    a. one thousand dollars ☐

    b. four hundred dollars ☐

    c. one thousand two hundred dollars. ☐

7. Buck pulled the sled for…

    a. forty meters. ☐

    b. seventy meters. ☐

    c. one hundred meters. ☐

6 Read pages 46–53. Are these sentences true or false? Write **T** or **F**.

1. Thornton, Hans and Pete went to the far east of the Yukon to look for gold. `T`

2. They traveled for two years. ☐

3. There was never enough food to eat. ☐

4. The pool in the valley was full of yellow butter. ☐

5. When they got to the valley the dogs could relax and rest. ☐

6. Buck started going into the forest for many days. ☐

7. One day when he came back to the camp, the men and the dogs were dead. ☐

8. Buck killed three of the men. The other man ran into the trees. ☐

AFTER READING ACTIVITIES

1 Complete the sentences with a word from the box.

> argued   ax   break   huskies
> limped   mountains   rope   whip

1. Thornton's leg hurt badly and he __limped__ for a long time.
2. There are some very high _____ in the Yukon.
3. The man put a _____ on Buck and pulled it hard.
4. A team of _____ pulled the sled from Skagway to Dawson.
5. Mercedes and the men _____ all day and most of the evening.
6. Perrault only hit the dogs with the _____ when it was needed.
7. Dolly was killed with an _____.
8. The men knew the trail was fast and they wanted to _____ a record.

2 Match the beginnings and endings of these sentences.

1. Manuel took Buck
2. Life in the Yukon
3. Perrault saw this was a great chance
4. Buck was the leader of the team now
5. Dave didn't want to be out of his harness
6. They pulled as hard as they could
7. "Don't go on the ice, it's too thin,"
8. Then Buck took Thornton's hand in his mouth

a. to break a record and make some money.
b. but they still couldn't move the sled.
c. because he was proud of his work.
d. because he liked to bet and needed money.
e. was very different from life at Mr. Miller's.
f. he told them.
g. and moved his head from side to side.
h. and the other dogs knew it.

3. Look at each picture and answer the questions.

1. Where is Buck? What is he doing?

   He is at Mr. Miller's house. He is carrying Mr. Miller's sons on his back.

2. What has Spitz done?

3. Why does François have his arms around Buck?

4. Who are these two men?

5. Why is Buck pulling the sled?

6. Why is Buck angry with this man?

4 Do the crossword.

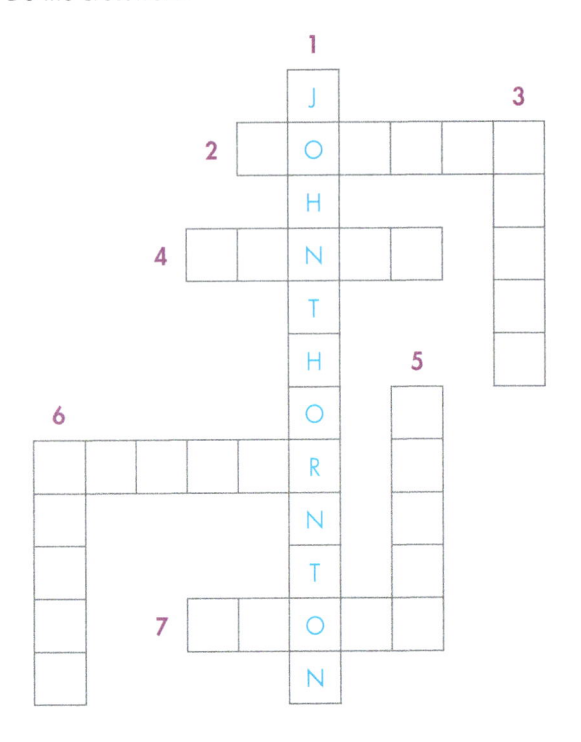

Down

1. Buck loves this man.
3. Buck becomes this when he lives in the Yukon.
5. Perrault calls Spitz this.
6. Perrault wanted to beat the record because the dogs were rested and the sled was…

Across

2. Buck meets these in the forest.
4. These are in your body. You can break them.
6. Spitz is this, but Buck wants to be this.
7. The noise a dog makes when it's angry.

5 Who says these words in the story?
1. "If he gives you trouble just pull the rope hard."
   Manuel.

2. "That Spitz is a devil. He's going to kill Buck one day."
   _____

3. "He wants to die at work."
   _____

4. "Please don't hit them! If you hit them again, I won't come with you."
   _____

5. "If you hit that dog again, I'll kill you."
   _____

6. "But I don't think he can do it, John."
   _____

7. "The ice on the ground is holding the sled. He'll have to break that ice first."
   _____

6 Answer the questions.
1. Do you think Buck is happier at the end of the story than at the beginning? Give reasons for your answer.
2. What do we learn in the story about men and dogs? Do the men love their dogs, or do they only care about finding gold?
3. All the other dogs in Buck's team die. Only Buck lives. Why is this?
4. What important things does Buck learn when he's in the Yukon?
5. *In a second, Buck knew it. This was going to be a fight to the end.* How does Buck know this?
6. Why is Buck a good lead dog?
7. *He also knew that the two men and the woman were no good and couldn't learn.* Why does Buck think this about Hal, Charles, and Mercedes?
8. Why does Buck love John Thornton?

GLOSSARY

argue speak angrily to someone

ax a big knife for cutting trees

bark make a noise like a dog

bear a big, dangerous wild animal

bet risk money by trying to guess what will happen

bite cut with your teeth

bone the hard, white parts inside an animal's or person's body

break a record do something faster or better than anyone else

camp a place where someone lives for a short time

club a heavy stick

devil a dangerous person or animal

excited nervous and happy

experienced good at something because you have done it many times

frightened afraid because something is dangerous

ground the hard earth

growl make a low noise in the throat

harness a leather and metal object that you put on a working animal

howl make a high long noise like a dog or a wolf

husky a large strong dog which can pull sleds

leader the most important person or animal

lick touch something with your tongue

life the activities that are part of the way somebody or something lives

limp walk slowly because one leg or foot hurts

mountain a very high hill

pool a small area of water

rabbit a small animal with long ears

respect think highly of someone

rope a long, thick string

scream give a loud, high cry

shoulder the top of the arm

sled something for traveling over snow, often pulled by dogs

smart intelligent and able to think quickly

stupid not intelligent and slow to learn

tent a house made of material that you can carry from place to place

whip a long thin piece of rope with a handle, used for making animals move

wolf (plural **wolves**) a large wild animal in the dog family

StandFor Readers

StandFor Readers provide a range of extensive reading materials for learners of all ages. The readers are carefully selected to cater for a range of interests, and are available across nine levels. Each title is meticulously graded for both vocabulary and structure, and topics have been selected to reflect the age and ability of students. Standfor Graded Readers are graded according to the Common European Framework of Reference for Languages (CEFR). Factual titles respond to the need for Content and Language Integrated Learning materials.

StandFor Young Readers

Level 1 — 125 Headwords
- The Enormous Turnip
- Little Red Hen
- The Three Little Pigs
- Katie's Camera

Level 2 — 240 Headwords
- The Cats and the Fishes
- The Gingerbread Man
- The Three Hungry Goats
- Peach Boy

Level 3 — 390 Headwords
- The Emperor's New Clothes
- The Little Prince
- Little Red Riding Hood
- The Town Mouse and the Country Mouse
- What Is Inside the Big Red Suitcase?

Level 4 — 540 Headwords
- Arachne
- Couscous
- Puss in Boots
- Transportation Around the World
- The Twelve Months

Level 5 — 680 Headwords
- Dragon Boat
- Icarus
- Let's Go to the City
- Nuala
- The Stories of King Arthur

StandFor Graded Readers

Level 1 — 380 Headwords — CEFR: A1
- The Adventures of Tom Sawyer
- Festivals
- Rip Van Winkle

Level 2 — 580 Headwords — CEFR: A2
- Great Navigators
- The Monkey's Paw
- Sherlock Holmes: The Yellow Band

Level 3 — 800 Headwords — CEFR: A2
- The Black Cat and Other Stories
- Oceans
- The Ransom of Red Chief and Other Stories

Level 4 — 1000 Headwords — CEFR: B1
- The Call of the Wild
- Climate Change
- Robinson Crusoe